Scottish Ghosts and Witches

The Haunted Explorer Series: Book 2

G Stewart

ISBN-13: 978-1492139201

ISBN-10: 1492139203

This book is dedicated to my family,
for never discouraging me from my
beliefs and for all their
help and support.

Contents

About the Author 7

St Monans Church and Newark Castle, Fife 9

The Witch's Grave, Kilrenny 14

Pittenweem Tolbooth Tower, Fife (Revisited) 15

The Phantom Piper, St Andrews 23

Dunino Church and Den, Fife 25

About Orbs 31

Balmerino Abbey, Fife 36

Ravenscraig Castle, Kirkcaldy 39

Lordscairnie Castle, Fife 42

MacDuff Castle, East Wemyss 44

Fyvie Castle, Aberdeenshire 47

Glenfinnan Viaduct, Highlands 51

Fort William Library, Highlands 53

Delgatie Castle, Aberdeenshire 54

The House of Terror, No.17, Edinburgh 57

The Royal Mile, Edinburgh 59

Loch Ness and the Monster 69

Other Title available 76

Author Details 80

About the Author

Before I share my experiences, I think it is appropriate to give a little information about myself. I am a 40 something year old professional, but since an early age I have been passionate about all things supernatural and mythology. It fascinates me that these stories have been passed down from generation to generation, and the sheer number of people who claim to have encountered similar things in similar locations.

I also love old buildings and over the years, I have visited many of them. On some occasions I know the location is reputedly haunted and I am essentially visiting wanting to experience the atmosphere, but a lot of the time when visiting these historic places, I am not aware of any stories nor am I looking for anything paranormal, I'm just looking at the building with it's historic significance in mind. Even so, I always take a lot of photographs and every now and again, something I can't quite explain shows up.

I don't consider myself to have any real psychic abilities, but I do believe I have a high level of intuition. I can generally read people quite easily, and often get a gut feeling when something is going to happen, and it then does. This carries across to when I'm a visiting place, and I just get a feeling that something is not all it appears to be. That said, I remain an open-minded sceptic. I believe there is something out there, something we do not yet fully understand, but I do not know what..... not yet!

Where possible, I have personally visited the locations covered in this book and my aim is to share my personal opinion and any photographic evidence I captured. I do not however aim to change anyone's views or try to convince them in any way, I am purely presenting my findings and I will leave the individuals to form their own opinion. I will always try to highlight the area of interest to try to make it as visible as possible.

St Monans Church and Newark Castle, Fife

The church in the picturesque fishing village of St Monans in Fife is an impressive sight. Rather than the more traditional cruciform shape, the church remains a T shape, but it is its location that makes it impressive. Considered to be the closest church to the sea in the country, the graveyard wall doubles up as the sea wall with the church building itself standing just a few meters back.

The origins of the church are steeped in history and myth. According to legend, either Saint Monan himself visited and established a chapel on the site in the 7th century or his bones were brought there and a shrine was constructed in his memory in the 9th century. It was claimed that the shrine held healing powers and in the 14th Century, King David II, son of Robert the Bruce, went to the site after being injured in battle. Despite one of his injuries being considered to be inoperable, upon visiting the chapel the wound healed and King David made a full recovery. To show his thanks, he ordered and funded the construction of the church to replace the chapel and work commenced in 1362. The church suffered considerable damage in the 16th Century during an attack by the English, but was rebuilt and then extensively renovated in the early 19th Century.

The church is reputedly haunted by a figure within the tower that was witnessed by a young man many years ago, who had been assigned the task of clearing out and re-lighting the furnace in the church. On one early morning, after completing his duties, the man's eye was drawn to a light high up in the tower. As he watched, he realised there was a face within the light staring back at him and, in terror, he fled and ran to the minister's house. While telling the minister what happened, he noticed a painting hanging on the wall of the minister's house and immediately recognised it as the face that he had witnessed in the church just a few minutes before. There is some variance in the story as to the identity of the person in the painting. Some say it was the minister's deceased wife, while another version states that it was David Leslie, 1st Lord of Newark.

David Leslie was a highly successful military commander and a prominent figure in the English and Scottish civil wars from 1640. In 1651 he led a Scottish Royalist force, fighting on behalf of Charles II of England into battle against the Parliamentarian forces, led by Oliver Cromwell, at the battle of Worcester. Leslie's forces were greatly outnumbered and were defeated, with Leslie being captured and held prisoner in the notorious Tower of London.

When Charles II was restored to the throne in 1660, he released Leslie, who returned to Scotland with a sizeable sum of money that had been paid to him by the king for his services to the Royalist Cause. Leslie returned to purchased Newark Castle, which he had bought in 1649 and stands approximately one third of a mile from St Monans Church, and King Charles II awarded him the title of the 1st Lord of Newark. He set about extensively remodelling the castle and it is thought that the ruins of the castle as they stand today are the remains of the building modelled by David Leslie. A castle has however stood on the site since the 13th Century.

It is believed the original castle was constructed on behalf of Sir Alan Durward, an important political figure of the 13th Century and who is also named as being responsible for the construction of the shrine to Saint Monan. This would presumably have been a replacement to any building previously built and, if this were the case, it would be the shrine Durward constructed that King David visited, which gives a link between the church and the castle.

There are reports of a spectral figure being seen at Newark Castle, which many believe to be a smuggler, but one can't help but wonder if it may in fact be David Leslie, given his strong connections with the castle. To add to this possibility, upon his death in 1682, Leslie was buried at St Monans Church, and it seems his body was disturbed during the restoration work in the 19th Century. It is not clear what happened to his remains after this incident

Newark Castle is an interesting place to visit and well worth the walk along the coastal path from St Monans, even just to view it from the outside due to its dangerous condition. I took many photographs during my visit, and the following showed a strange anomaly in one of the openings, which appears to be a face looking up from the lower ground level within the room the opening serves. My initial feelings were that this was simply changes in the texture of the stonework for the inner wall, however, I took several photographs of this area in quick succession, and this the only one in which this appeared, which I find curious.

Newark Castle

The possible face is at the bottom of the opening. The streaks of light in the photograph are rain.

St Monans church is also connected with witchcraft. During the period of the witch trials, a young lady named Maggie Morgan caught the eye of one of the Anstruther family members. The Anstruther family were at the time one of the most powerful families in Scotland, and were later involved in the passing of the Act of the Union in 1707, which joined the Kingdoms of Scotland and England to form the United Kingdom of Great Britain. It seems however Maggie was not influenced by the importance of the family, or did not know whom the young man was, and she turned down his advances.

A short while later, Maggie was accused of 'taking up' with a witch from nearby Pittenweem who had taught her evil spells and, after being given almost no trial, she was convicted and sentenced to death. She was burned

12

at the stake in 1650 and her ashes were arranged around the steeple at St Monans church to allow them to be blown into the surrounding consecrated ground. If the figure that has been seen in the church tower is indeed a woman, perhaps it is young Maggie.

St Monans association with Witchcraft started centuries before Maggie Morgan was accused, with the legend of Witch Grizzie. In the 15th Century, Witch Grizzie was convicted of witchcraft and sentenced to be burnt at the stake. While waiting for the sentence to be carried out, Witch Grizzie was allowed to fall asleep and as soon as she did, she transformed into a droning beetle. She was never again seen in human form. but those who were involved with her conviction were plagued for the rest of their life with a droning noise in their ears. After this incident, those accused of witchcraft were not allowed to sleep after being convicted.

The Witch's Grave, Kilrenny, Fife

The village of Kilrenny lies in the East Neuk of Fife, not far from the fishing town of Anstruther. In my youth I was told the story of the witch's grave, and shown it in the village graveyard.

The 'grave' was in fact a stone trough in the ground, with a pool of water collected in it from recent rainfall. I was told that an old woman who lived in the village and whom everyone feared was a witch was buried there. The trough was created above her as it would naturally fill with rainwater and slowly drain through cracks in the stonework, creating a pool of slow-moving water. As witches are said to be unable to cross moving water, the trough would ensure she could never rise from her resting place.

Whether there is any truth in the story I do not know, however I did recently return to the graveyard to find out the name of the person buried there to do some research, and I found that the trough had been filled in with soil and a tree planted! If this was indeed an unmarked witch's grave, there is nothing to prevent her returning now!

Pittenweem Tolbooth Tower – Revisited

Pittenweem Tolbooth Tower

The following history and background relating to the Tolbooth Tower is taken from my earlier book, 'Scotland's Hidden Hauntings'. For those who have already read the earlier book and do not wish to read about the towers past again, please go to the update which starts on page 20.

At the end of the high street of the picturesque fishing village of Pittenweem in the East Neuk of Fife, stands the Tolbooth tower, a four-storey building with a

15

vaulted basement. The tower as it stands today was built in the 1620s... although there was probably a building on the site previously.

Many people looking at the tower understandably assume it is just part of the adjoining church, but the Tolbooth has had an unsavoury past which I first became aware of when friends suggested going on the Weem Witch tour, organised by local historian Leonard Low. Leonard has written the book 'The Weem Witch', which tells the true story of the witch trials in Pittenweem in 1704, and the horrific brutality that took place within the walls of the Tolbooth. Having contacted Leonard, we arranged to attend the next tour.

The Tolbooth itself is a tower with a steep spiral staircase and essentially one room per floor. Leonard's tour was to tell the history of the events that took place in the tower rather than a 'ghost tour', although we were warned to be careful with electronic equipment such as cameras as batteries have a tendency to drain of power or cameras simply stop working all together within the tower. Once we were inside, Leonard began to tell us what took place surrounding the 1704 witch trials.

Pittenweem at that time was a wealthy town, but all that was to change. The men of the town had been sent to assist in the battle against the Jacobites with very few returning, and most of the fishing fleet had been destroyed during a storm. The town authorities needed to raise money to repair the damage caused to the harbour by the storm and rebuild the fishing boats, but with few men left to work in the village and no income from fishing, this was proving impossible. But in March

1704, Patrick Morton, a sixteen year old blacksmith, presented the authorities with an opportunity. After an argument with a wealthy local lady, Beatrix Laing, Morton found a bucket with water and fire coal at his door. He fell ill shortly after, suffering from fits, and accused Bearix Laing of using witchcraft against him in retribution for their argument. Beatrix was arrested and brought to the Tolbooth for questioning. The town council at the time met in the room on the first floor, which is where she was initially taken for the charges to be put to her, but after refusing to sign a confession she was taken to the second floor, where the torture began. Methods commonly used were 'walking the witch', whereby the accused would have a rope tied around them and they would be walked round the room by the guards. Though the guards would take breaks and take turns to 'walk the witch', the accused was not allowed to rest, received no food or water and would sometimes be walked for days at a time. If they slowed, they would be struck with a bat, which would often have nails driven through it to rip flesh from the body.

The most dreaded means of torture was however delivered by the Witch Prickers. The accused would first of all be stripped naked and every hair shaved from their body. They would then be examined for any unusual markings, as the belief was that a witch would have a devil's mark, which would confirm they had been touched by Satan. This mark could be anything, many of which occur naturally on the human body such as moles or scars. It was however believed that the witch would feel no pain at the devil's mark and it would not bleed, and so to test this the Witch Pricker would drive a needle or spike, several inches long, into the mark. If the accused showed any sign of pain, this was taken as evidence that it was not a devil's mark that had been found, and the examination would continue. If by some miracle the accused managed not to show their pain, they were considered a witch and sent for execution.

If, after every blemish on the body had been tested and the devil's mark had still not been found, rather than consider the accused to be innocent, it was assumed the mark must be hidden under the skin. The Pricker would then start to drive his needle into every inch of the body of the accused, looking for a spot where they felt no pain. This process could take days and many of those accused gave up and admitted to witchcraft just to end their agony. At the time, a confession obtained through torture was only accepted if it was backed up by a second confession provided at the free will of the accused. After the first confession, the accused would then be made comfortable, fed and treated well, before being asked to sign the second confession. Many by this time had come to their senses, and refused to do so, at which point they were taken back upstairs for the Pricker to go to work on them again. It really was a hopeless situation and eventually most of the accused signed both confessions, but as well as confessing, they were asked to name other people in the village who also practiced witchcraft. In desperation to stop the torture, each of the accused provided several names of others, normally friends or neighbours, who were then brought to the Tolbooth and subjected to the same process until they confessed.

Once the confessions had been obtained, the 'witches' were burned at the stake in an area just outside the village. The authorities, led by the local minister Patrick

Cowper, then seized all possessions of the accused, including their houses, and the family would be billed for their relative's time held in captivity, the Pricker's time, and even the wood for the fire to burn them! Good fortune ensured that the initial person accused was wealthy, meaning the people she was likely to name as also being witches would also be wealthy, ensured a sizeable income for the authorities.

By the time the trials ended in 1705, twenty-six people had been accused and tortured, and eighteen had been killed. The most horrific case was that of Janet Cornfoot, whom Laing had named. Janet became a 'problem' for Cowper as she had spoken to a visiting official from the ruling City of Edinburgh regarding her treatment within the Tolbooth. That night she seemingly managed to escape through a second floor window. Bearing in mind she had been tortured for days, much speculation surrounds her escape as not only would she have needed to leap from a second floor window, she would have had to avoid the guards and get past the town wall. It is thought she may have been released to 'remove the problem' with the Edinburgh officials for Cowper. She was however captured around ten miles away and returned to Pittenweem. She was immediately met by an angry mob, who subjected her to beatings and dragged her down to the harbour, where she was tied to a rope and repeatedly submerged in the ice cold water. She escaped into a nearby house, but the mob threatened the occupants and pulled the door off its hinges. The door was put on top of Janet and stones piled on top until the weight crushed her to death. To make sure she was dead, a sledge used to pull goods from the harbour up to the village was run over her body several times.

After discovering the truth about the trials and writing 'The Weem Witch', Leonard started to run the tours of the Tolbooth as a historical tour, but soon after things started to happen in the tower. These have included people feeling nauseous and having to leave, people being scratched, unexplained sounds coming from empty areas of the tower, and sightings of figures. Several people have ended up requiring medical treatment following their experience in the tower.

Update

I have visited the tower on many occasions, always taking part in the tours when I can. As I have always felt there is something there and having captured a number of images of light anomalies, I jumped at the opportunity to spend time in the tower without the organised tours. A fellow investigator and myself, armed with digital voice recorders, cameras, electro-magnetic field meters (EMF meters) and a trigger object, planned to spend up to six hours in the tower. Unfortunately that was not to be the case. In the first hour we spent time in each of the main rooms, starting at the top floor and working our way down. The EMF meter activated a number of times while we were standing still in the rooms, and we had the digital voice recorder running. After this sweep we went outside for a break for around twenty minutes before heading back in to repeat the process. As soon as we walked in we felt something had changed; the atmosphere was heavier and far more intimidating. However, it was also darker so we headed up to the third floor to start over again. The EMF meter started to pick up on changes in the electro-magnetic field again for a few minutes at a time, with pauses in-between with nothing. We both had the feeling of being watched from the stairs and there were numerous bangs coming from the stairs, although we could not exclude the possibility of the wind causing this. A name came to us, and when we called out for it things went a bit crazy, with a stone being thrown at us! We were both constantly seeing shadows move on the stairs and started to feel uncomfortable. We did manage to find an explanation for some of the noises though when we discovered a pigeon nesting on one of the windowsills higher up the tower, which was tapping the glass every time it moved!

After about an hour we moved to the room on the second floor, and again repeated the process. We continued to witness shadows on the stairs, as well as lights. Interestingly one of us saw one of the flashes as an orange light while the other saw it as blue. We experienced feelings of light-headedness and the feeling of being touched. We went down to the first floor room, one that has always felt calmer (this room was used for meetings whereas the 2nd and 3rd floor rooms were used for torturing the accused), but even in this room we were uncomfortable. Just over three hours after we first entered the tower, we left.

Despite taking numerous photographs, nothing showed up other than some orbs, which could have been dust. The digital voice recorder, however, gave a lot more evidence. There are lots of whispers in the background throughout, but in the final recording, four minutes before we decided to leave the second floor room, there is a growling voice saying 'get out'. This is repeated shortly after, although not as loudly. The most impressive recording was captured a few minutes before we felt we had to leave the tower. We had been asking whether whoever remained in the tower objected to the tours taking place, and a response is given saying 'Definitely......too much talking.' There is then a final word, which we initially thought was 'Janet has,' but it has now been suggested that it is 'Jesus' in Latin. Our voices on the recording are fairly faint, but the voice which replies is louder, indicating it was closer to the voice recorder than we were, despite it being in my hand! It also talks over us. This recording was taken on the second floor of the tower, when no one else was there. The recording can be listened to by entering the following web address on a computer. The recording is looped and repeated four times for clarity.

http://www.youtube.com/watch?v=lXMTWRBFxeU

Without a doubt, this is the most uncomfortable experience with the paranormal I have had. I was physically drained for several hours after, feeling as though all my energy had been taken from me, and my joints ached (it has been said before that whatever is in the tower targets people's weaknesses, and I have problems with my joints). When checking the details afterwards, the name that came to us, 'William', was a prominent figure in the witch trials and, although we believe he showed deep remorse for his involvement later in his life, we wonder whether it was William who did not like being identified and wanted us to leave. This also fits in with it being William who responded saying he objects to the tours due to there being too much talking. He is unlikely to want the events he regrets being involved in repeatedly told to a new audience. One thing is for sure, we will be returning!

The Phantom Piper, St Andrews, Fife

It is said that there is a cave between the Castle Sands and the Harbour in St Andrews, which gives access to a tunnel. When the tunnel was discovered, the authorities sent a piper into it with the instructions to play his pipes as he walked. The intention was that this would allow the piper's progress to be checked above ground and by following the sound of the pipes, the route of the tunnel could be found. However, after around five minutes, the pipes went silent. Search parties were sent in to find out what happened to the piper, but no trace of him was ever found and what happened to him remains a mystery. As time passed his family continued to search for him, with some claiming his wife also became lost in the caves, but he was never found. When the area on top of the cliffs between the castle and the cathedral was eventually built upon, forming the street called the East Scores, the resultant construction work resulted in many of the openings in the caves beneath being covered.

Residents who moved into the properties soon however began to report hearing pipes playing on stormy nights. Some claimed to also witness a lone piper walking along a section of cliffs where it would be impossible to walk, and this led to speculation and tales that the ghost of the piper had returned to continue his task.

This is the type of story I am always wary of, as it exists in many places, such as the phantom piper in Edinburgh who reportedly went missing doing the same thing following a tunnel from the castle down the Royal Mile. However, to possibly add some credibility to the stories of these tunnels, the remains of the ancient 'David's Tower' were discovered during excavation works beneath Edinburgh Castle in the early 20th Century, and more recently trenches have been discovered beneath the castle. Indeed perhaps there is more to these tales of secret tunnels; it's just that the buildings they lead from are no longer there.

In St Andrews, there are numerous claims of secret tunnels connecting the castle and the cathedral and onto the harbour, where a boat could be kept moored to allow the authorities of that time a means for quick escape if attacked.The location of the tunnel in which the piper is claimed to have gone missing would fit in with these supposedly long lost escape tunnels, with the 'entrance' being well positioned for escape to sea. Thus, if the tunnel did exist, what is described as the 'entrance' may have in fact been the exit of an escape tunnel from the castle, the cathedral, or both. My grandfather once told me, before I knew of the story of the phantom piper, that as a child he had discovered a cave in the area of the West Cliffs in St Andrews. Inside he found a rusted steel gate at the back, preventing access to a narrow cavern behind. Perhaps this could have been the tunnel the piper was lost in.

Dunino Den and Church, Fife

In my youth I was told a tale relating to the area around Dunino Church. Several hundred years ago a weary traveller looking for the church took a wrong turn and came upon a tiny hamlet of just a few houses. Outside one of the houses an elderly couple stood in silence, staring at the traveller who, feeling something was not right with the situation he had found himself in, turned without asking for directions and headed back the way he came. After finding the path to the church, the traveller went about his business and later commented on the hamlet he had found himself in earlier in the day only to be met by puzzled looks. There was no hamlet in the area in which he mentioned, and records showed there had never been any houses there. It seems the traveller's instincts were correct about the village and he was no doubt forever grateful he did not approach the elderly couple. I recall being told the church was near the 'Druid's Den' but with the innocence of my youth, a Druid to me symbolised a wizard type figure, and I left it at that.

As I grew up I learned more about Druids, who are the priests of a religious order amongst the Celts, who first arrived in Britain around 1500 BC. Very few verifiable facts are known about the ancient Druids as they did not keep written records, and so much of what is written about them is based on accounts from other sources and archaeological evidence. I have now visited the den, which is accessed from a path which runs down the side of the church yard, on several occasions. Two rocky outcrops look out over the den, one complete with a pool and footprint carved into the solid rock. It is likely this is a sacrificial pool, with the blood being drained into the pool before the body was thrown over the edge of the outcrop into the river directly below. There is a possibility this included human sacrifices.

The Sacrficial Pool, Dura Den

Steep steps carved into the rock face lead down into the den itself, where there are a number of symbols carved, including a Celtic cross of around ten feet tall. Although heavily worn, most of the cross remains. The entire area of the den remains covered in ribbons tied to the trees, painted shells and wicker symbols, presumably all left for religious reasons. The rock face is covered in coins that have been inserted into cracks to bring good luck. Beneath the second rock outcrop is a small opening, just large enough for a small human to fit inside. This seems to go into the rock for around two meters before turning at right angles to lead further into the rock. I could not fit in myself to see how far back the opening went, and I am not sure if I would have wanted to. Something felt very sinister about this opening. My impression in the purpose of this outcrop, which has a flat top and overlooks the main part of the den, was that this was where the high priest conducted the religious services. This platform-like outcrop looks directly across to the outcrop with the sacrificial pool, and I wonder if the opening beneath could have been where the animals, or even humans, were kept prior to being led across the den and up the stairs to be sacrificed. I took a number of photographs in this opening and in a smaller opening above, and a strange light anomaly showed up in one of them, as shown in the following picture;

Orb at Dura Den

Although this may be deemed another orb and easily explained, I took several photographs in this area in quick succession and this is the only photograph where anything out of the ordinary appeared. In addition, I find the solid form of the orb to be unusual if it was simply an insect or dust. I have since confirmed the opening does open up into a small cavern and revisited the area with an expert in the history of witchcraft, who is of the opinion that this is likely to be where the 'wise woman' (the healer) of the community would have lived.

The area around the den is also connected with witchcraft. A young girl named Alison Pearson, who lived a short distance from the den, is said to have fallen ill as a child. Her deceased cousin, who appeared to her in the form of a Green Man, visited her and told her that he could make her well again if she would be faithful to him. She was then transported to the Faerie world where she was taught how to heal through the use of herbal remedies. It should be noted that the Faeries in folklore are very different from the 'fairy' made famous by the likes of Disney movies. In Folklore, the Faerie is a supernatural being that was not to be crossed. Described by some as being too evil to enter Heaven but being too good to enter Hell, the Faeries stayed somewhere in the middle. They are considered to be mischievous, though not necessarily malicious, as long as they are left alone. They are believed to be capable of powerful magic and responsible for leading travellers deep into forests where they become lost, and also for acting as 'changelings', where a person would be kidnapped in the woods and held captive while a Faerie would take the form of the person and be sent out into the world in their place. Faeries are believed to live in hollow hills, known as Faerie Mounds, and, particularly in Ireland, it is considered unlucky to disturb these mounds or to block the Faerie paths leading to them. People have been known to remove corners from their properties if they block a Faerie path and many properties which do cross a path were built so the front and back door are in line with each other, along the line of the Faerie path, so the doors can be left open to allow the Faeries to pass through undisturbed. These may seem drastic steps, but they demonstrate what people are prepared to do to avoid the wrath of the Faeries.

Shortly after her cousin visited her, Alison made a full recovery and went on to become a very well known healer through the use of herbs, and grew to become known as a 'wise woman' for her healing abilities. Eventually she was called upon to help Patrick Adamson, Archbishop of St Andrews, Fife. She treated Adamson in St Andrews castle and through her remedies cured him of what was described as 'a serious illness'. Using her abilities to cure a man as well known as Adamson, who had many enemies, led to fatal consequences for Alison. She was accused of witchcraft, and unfortunately as soon as she was accused, her fate was sealed. She stood no chance with a jury made up of mainly men of the church, and even if he wanted to, Adamson could not speak up in her defence, as the witchcraft act passed in 1563 by Mary Queen of Scots stated:

'Nor that na persoun seik ony help, response or casultatioun at ony sic usaris or abusaris foir saidis of Witchcraftis, Sorsareis or Necromancie, under the pane of deid, alsweill to be execute aganis the usar, abusar,

as the seikar of the response or consultatioun.'

Roughly translated, this act states that any person who sought help, consultation or assisted a witch was also guilty by association and would suffer the pain of death. Thus, Adamson could not admit knowingly consulting a possible witch or offer her any assistance or he too would face certain death. Unsurprisingly, Alison Pearson was found guilty of witchcraft and burned at the stake in Edinburgh in 1588.

The one part I found particularly interesting regarding this story was the connection with a Green Man. The symbol of the Green Man can be found in many locations throughout Britain and is generally a face surrounded by foliage forming the hair and beard. Green Men are thought to be spirits of the wood, a symbol of the rebirth of nature and the life that can be found in the plant world, which would fit in with the claims that Alison Pearson was taught, via a Green Man, to use herbs for her remedies. It is also claimed that she picked her herbs in the area around Dunino Church, which is also where the Druid Den lies. During my first visit to the den, I found a carving of what appears to be a Green Man in the rock face. It has been worn away over the years, indicating it is very old, and I can't help but wonder if this symbol, in such an ancient, mystical place, is related to the tale of Alison Pearson. A photograph of this Green Man carving has been used as the cover for this book.

About Orbs

Given that I have stated I am not a great believer of the theory that orbs are evidence of the supernatural, it may seem strange that I have then gone on to show a number of photographs of orbs. I think it seems appropriate to give some more information on this subject.

Orbs are balls of light which became the new phenomena of ghost hunting in the 1990s as digital cameras started to replace traditional film cameras. Many speculated that the different way in which the photograph was captured allowed previously unseen parts of the image to be seen, and that these orbs were the first manifestation of a spirit. Others pointed out that it was simply the flash being closer to the lens, resulting in dust, insects and moisture being visible in a way it did not previously show up on film. I have to agree that the vast majority of photographs showing orbs are simply dust etc. Despite using some photographs of orbs in this book, I have discounted literally thousands of other photographs I have taken showing orbs. To believe that every photograph showing an orb shows something paranormal would mean believing that there are hundreds of unseen spirits walking beside us at all times, which I don't.

The following photograph is an example of one of the many I have discounted;

'Orbs' at Niddry Street Vaults

This photograph shows the stone circle in the former witches' temple at the Niddry Street Vaults. Edinburgh's underground vaults are covered in the book 'Scotland's Hidden Hauntings' and are considered to have one of the highest levels of paranormal activity in the world. The stone circle is said to contain a particularly malevolent spirit, trapped by the witches who used to worship there (they still do, but have moved their temple to what they consider a safer vault) and visitors are warned not to stand in the circle. It would therefore be easy to imagine that the photograph may have captured an image of this evil spirit, but before such a conclusion can be made, many other things must be considered.

On this visit to the vaults, there was a high level of moisture in the air. The orbs look similar, with central spots and outer rings, which would indicate a flash glare. Taking into account these observations alone, along with the number of orbs in the photograph, there was sufficient information for me to discount the photograph.

Apart from the obvious questions, such as 'was a flash used?' or 'was it daylight?', there are several things I look out for in orbs. First is how solid the orb is. While true sceptics will argue that a solid orb is formed due to an airborne particle being very close to the lens, I look at the surroundings, which gives a better idea of how far away the orb is before I decide if it is worth considering further. The density of the orb is another factor, with many believing what we see as light is actually pure energy, and I find images where the density varies to be interesting. I also consider the colour of the orb. Colour does not immediately mean it is paranormal. It is important to consider your surroundings and the environment you are in, as different particles can reflect as different colours; for example, pollen can show up as yellow, and some particles such as water can allow varying amounts of the light spectrum to shine through creating the appearance of variations in the colour of the orb. The final thing I consider is whether I saw the orb with my own eyes or only in the photograph after.

Looking back at the photograph shown earlier, there are two orbs that did stand out, both to the left of shot. The first orb is close to the top of the vault;

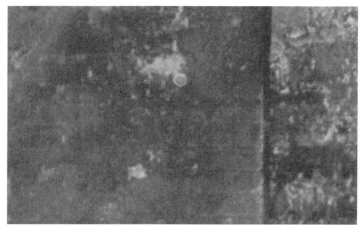

'Orb' at Niddry Street Vaults

The semi-solid structure and coloured rings in this orb caught my eye, as it is unusual in appearance.

The second one is close to the left hand wall, just above the step;

'Orb' at Niddry Street Vaults

This orb is very small, and appears to be solid and blue in colour. In the underground vaults it is very unlikely that any airborne particle is going to be anything other than dust, moisture, or a flying insect, and none of these could be expected to appear as a solid blue circle.

Readers may therefore wonder why I have discounted the photograph. The first orb was discounted due to the surroundings. In the main photograph it can be seen that the only light source in the vault was a candle on the back wall. It is therefore likely that this orb is simply a water droplet with the burning flame behind showing through.

The second orb is more difficult to explain, but must be taken in context with the rest of the image. Looking at the photograph as a whole and the number of other natural occurring orbs, along with the small size and quality of the close-up photograph, it is also difficult to discount it being something natural. It is only after I have discounted, or at least minimised, the likelihood of normal sources for the orb that I consider the possibility of a paranormal source. Where I have used photographs of orbs, I always try to explain why.

Balmerino Abbey, Fife

Balmerino Abbey

Balmerino Abbey lies on the edge of the small village of Balmerino by the River Tay. According to the details of the building's listing with Historic Scotland, the church in the abbey was founded in 1226, although building work on the site carried on for many years after and, as is common with many churches and religious buildings, it was a cruciform building. It was established as a Cistercian Abbey by the monks at Melrose Abbey in the Scottish Borders and housed up to twenty monks. In 1547 the Abbey was attacked by invading English forces and extensively damaged. It was repaired, but suffered far worse damage in the reformation when followers of John Knox destroyed the abbey, killing all of the monks that remained. Following the creation of the peerage with the title 'Lord of Balmerino', the remains of the abbey and its grounds formed part of the geographical barony of the first Lord of Balmerino, James Elphinstone, in 1604.

Today the Abbey remains in a ruinous condition, with the church building fenced off due to its dangerous condition.

The ghosts of the murdered monks are said to still roam the grounds with many reports of their spectral figures being witnessed pushing wheelbarrows as though continuing with their day-to-day chores. Another spirit which is said to haunt the abbey is reported to be seen sitting in the cellars, and is thought to be a monk who was responsible for keeping a watch on the corn stored in the cellars to ensure rats and mice did not eat it.

I have visited the abbey on several occasions and the only cellars that I know of which still remain are those of the Abbot's House, situated to the rear of the grounds. It is difficult to imagine that these cellars once belonged to what was probably a grand house, as they now appear to simply be part of a mound of earth:

Abbot's House, Balmerino Abbey

Of the many photographs I have taken in the abbey, one stands out which was taken in these cellars. It shows an orb, but what makes this orb different and difficult to explain by a natural occurrence is it does not directly face the camera, but appears to be turned at an angle making a reflection from the flash very unlikely. Could this be the spirit of the monk still watching for mice and rats in the cellar?

Orb at Balmerino Abbey

Ravenscraig Castle, Kirkcaldy, Fife

Ravenscraig Castle

Situated on a rocky outcrop between Kirkcaldy and Dysart lies Ravenscraig Castle. Work on the formidable building started in 1460, based on plans by King James II and funded by his widow, Mary of Guelders, with work being completed approximately four years later. The sea cliffs on three sides naturally defend the castle, with a deep dry ditch to the landside. The castle comprises of two D-shaped towers, connected by a cross range upon which guns were situated. The outer walls of the towers, at approximately fourteen feet thick, are designed to withstand cannon fire. Mary lived in the incomplete castle in the West Tower until her death in 1463, when ownership of the castle was passed to her son and then onto the Sinclair family, who finished construction of the castle. One of the roles of Ravenscraig Castle was to provide protection to merchant ships in the Firth of Forth against pirates who were situated on the nearby Isle of May.

Today the castle is a ruin with access to many of the rooms and upper levels closed off for safety reasons, but it remains easy to imagine how impressive it must have once been. It is considered a 'hidden gem' as a modern housing estate hides the castle from the road, but this means it is quieter than the better-known castles and well worth making the effort to visit. The ghost of a lady dressed in white has been seen wandering within the castle grounds, leading to speculation that it is the spirit of Mary of Guelders. However, the neighbouring housing estate stands on the site of an old hospital, and it is reported that children exploring the hospital building prior to its demolition witnessed the lady in white walking along the corridors. This has led others to believe that she is connected to the hospital, but used to visit the castle grounds that no doubt used to offer an area of peace and quiet, where hospital residents could benefit from the fresh sea air.

I have visited the castle on a couple of occasions. The higher levels used to be open to the public, but now that access has been closed it forms a number of dark openings. It is easy for your mind to play tricks with you here as it seems the information boards etc are still within the upper rooms, and so you do get glimpses of white within the darkness. I did take a number of photographs through an opening into a lower chamber of the West Tower, and in one a dark shadow and strange mist appeared;

Shadow Figure at Ravenscraig Castle

There is an orb in the photograph, but I believe that to be nothing other than dust or a flying insect. The shadow is directly to the left of the orb and appears to be surrounded by some form of swirling mist or distortion. The stonework for the wall behind can be seen through this mist.

Lordscairnie Castle

Lordscairnie Castle

Lordscairnie Castle is an 'L' shaped tower house which was built in the late 15th Century by the 7th Earl of Crawford, Sir Alexander Lindsay. The castle, which was once surrounded by a moat, has stood unoccupied since the mid 19th century and is now in a ruinous condition. From the above photograph it is difficult to believe the castle is still standing.

It is said that treasure is buried within the grounds of the castle in the form of money and valuables collected by the Earl. This treasure is commonly described as 'ill-gotten gains' and it is said that this was the reason the Earl buried it to keep it hidden. Many attempts have been made to find the treasure, especially when the moat was drained, but nothing of any significant value has been found....yet!

The castle is also reported to be haunted by Alexander Lindsay. It is said that he wished to plays cards on a Sunday, but with this being a Sabbath, no-one was prepared to play. Therefore, he declared that he would play with the Devil himself. The Devil appeared to him in human form and accepted the offer to play cards. Alexander was unaware of the true identity of the stranger and they played late into the night. Unfortunately for Alexander, the Devil won. His prize was Alexander's soul. It is said the card game is replayed every year on 31st December at the stroke of midnight and that when it finishes, anyone who witnessed it will be taken to hell with the Devil and the Earl.

A very similar story is told relating to the more famous Glamis Castle, with many speculating that it was the 4th Earl of Crawford, the 7th Earl's father, who played cards with the Devil at Glamis.

Despite its poor condition, Lordscairnie Castle is privately owned and therefore access is not permitted. It can however be viewed from the road and it is an atmospheric building. It is hoped that the castle will be restored to its former glory in the near future.

MacDuff Castle, East Wemyss, Fife

MacDuff Castle

The ruins of MacDuff Castle sits high on the cliff tops on the edge of the coastal village of East Wemyss. The current building dates back to the 14th century, however, it is likely a castle stood on the site prior to this, and the previous castle is connected with MacDuff, the Thane of Fife, more famous for being Macbeth's killer in the famous Shakespeare play 'Macbeth', although all traces of this castle are now gone.

The 14th century tower house was home to the Wemyss family. Sir Michael Wemyss had sworn allegiance to King Edward 1st of England, but during the Wars of Scottish Independence he changed allegiance to King Robert, the Bruce of Scotland. The castle was later destroyed by the English military, possibly under the direct order of King Edward. The land and castle was passed to another family and was repaired and extended to create a five-storey rectangular tower house with a spiral stair in a corner tower. The castle and lands came back into the ownership of the Wemyss family in the 17th Century, but by that time they were established in nearby Wemyss Castle and so MacDuff Castle was neglected and started to fall into a state of disrepair.

The castle today is extremely ruinous, with little remaining. It is possible to access the stair tower and take the steep steps either down to the dark basement or up to the top of the castle. Great care must be taken as at the top the walls have all collapsed, leaving the stairs exposed.

The ghost of Mary Sibbald haunts MacDuff Castle, a servant girl who was accused of being a petty thief and, after being found guilty, was sentenced to be flogged and unfortunately died from her injuries. Her ghost is seen wandering the castle grounds in the form of a grey lady, and her cries are also sometimes heard. I have visited MacDuff Castle on a number of occasions and every time I have the same feeling of being watched. In particular, I find the basement very unnerving. That said, despite its condition the castle remains an imposing building, and it is possibly simply that which creates the feeling of being watched.

The Wemyss family have not escaped spirits by moving properties. The ghost of a lady haunts Wemyss Castle, known as Green Jean due to her long, flowing green dress. A sighting of Green Jean is not something the family necessarily looks forward to however, as a common version of her story is that her presence warns that the current owner of the castle is approaching death.

Wemyss Castle is a private residence and public access is not permitted, however, as a child I did visit the grounds and the famous Wemyss Caves, which lie below the castle, on an organised trip, and it was then I first heard the story of Green Jean.

Fyvie Castle, Aberdeenshire

Fyvie Castle

Fyvie Castle sits in its own estate about twenty-five miles North of Aberdeen. One of the first things a visitor will notice is the sheer size of the castle. The earliest part of the castle dates back to the 13th century. It was then passed on through five clan families, each adding new towers and carrying out alterations resulting in the large scale and excellent architecture of the castle that we see today. Despite its splendour, the castle does however have a dark past, with many reports of it being haunted and a few curses placed upon it!

The first curse is attributed to Lady Meldrum, one of the first clan families to have lived at the castle. It is said that she requested that when she died, her remains should be kept in the walls of the castle and bad luck

47

would fall upon anyone who disturbed her. It seems this request was carried out as in the 1920s; workmen carrying out work on the property discovered a secret room with a woman's skeleton inside. Some reports have it that the Laird at the time asked for the remains to be removed and given a proper burial in the castle's churchyard. Almost immediately after, a number of strange and unexplained incidents started to occur, loud noises were heard around the castle, and a grey figure was seen walking around. The body was exhumed and returned to the secret room, which was sealed and remains sealed to this day. This seems to have stopped the strange occurrences around the castle associated with the grey lady, but she is still seen in the castle.

The second curse relates to another secret chamber within the castle, which lies beneath the Charter Room. It is said that if anyone enters the chamber, the laird of the castle will die and his wife will go blind. It is reported two lairds have tried to access the chamber; the first died and his wife went blind, just as the curse stated. The second started to feel unwell when he started to descend into the chamber, so sensibly he turned around and left. His wife however suffered from problems with her eyesight from that day onwards. The origin of the secret chamber and the purpose or what lies within don't seem to be very clear, and it is sometimes associated with the location where Lady Meldrum's body was sealed up.

A famous prophet, Thomas the Rhymer, also known as True Thomas due to his reputedly accurate prophecies, placed the final curse on the castle. According to the legend, Thomas was to visit the castle during his travels, and the gates had been left open pending his arrival. However, it was a particularly stormy night and when he arrived a gust of wind blew the gates shut. Thinking someone within the castle had slammed the gates shut in his face, he placed the curse of the weeping stones on the castle. The weeping stones are always wet irrespective of the weather or where they are, and he said there were three such stones within the castle and its grounds and as long as they remained within the grounds of the castle, no eldest son would succeed his father as laird of the castle. One of the stones has been found, and is kept in a bowl in the castle. It is a strange sight as, despite being kept inside in a relatively warm room, the stone is visibly soaking wet. Of the other two stones, one is said to be within the walls of the oldest tower, meaning it would be very difficult to find. The third stone however is said to be in the river on the grounds, where all the stones are naturally wet. To find out which stone in the river does not dry out when removed from the water would be an impossible task, and so the curse remains, and it is said that none of the laird's eldest sons have inherited the castle since.

A green lady, thought to be Dane Lilias Drummond, also haunts the castle. It is claimed that her husband, Sir Alexander Seaton, was keen to have a male heir, yet Lilias had given birth to five daughters. Lilias died suddenly while visiting the family home in Fife and Seaton very quickly turned his attentions towards Lady Grizel Leslie, and they were soon married. This led to speculation that Seaton had become so frustrated that his wife had not given him an heir that he had started an affair, leaving his wife broken-hearted.

On their wedding night, it is said that Alexander Seaton and his new wife Grizel were disturbed by knocking and scraping noises all night at the window of their bedroom. Knowing they were several floors above ground level, Seaton was keen to discount it as nothing but the wind, however, when he opened the curtains the following morning he discovered the name 'D Lilias Drummond' carved into the exterior of the stone windowsill. The carving can still be viewed today and many people have reported seeing the green lady walking the corridors of the castle.

The final ghost at the castle is a trumpeter, and it is said that the sound of him playing his trumpet foretells the death of the Laird of the Castle.

Fyvie is a very interesting castle to visit. Although it does seem that you do not get access to much of the building, access to the main areas associated with the legends are part of the tour. In two visits to the castle I have not captured any unusual images. We did however have an unusual incident on our first visit, at which point no one in our party knew any of the ghost stories associated with the castle. One of the younger members of our group started to run ahead and down the main staircase, at which point, fearful that they might fall on the large, spiral stairs, I called them back. When asked why, I replied, "Because there is a ghost on the stairs." After we had finished exploring the castle we visited the shop and I asked the shop assistant if the castle was haunted, at which point I was told about the stories covered here, including the grey lady, who we were informed was most commonly seen on the main staircase!

Glenfinnan Viaduct, Highlands

The West Highland Line is a train route which connects the City of Glasgow with the ports of Oban and Mallaig, with the final section running from Fort William in the Highlands to coastal town of Mallaig. The route is acknowledged to be one of the most scenic routes in the country, passing through stunning countryside, and the atmosphere is added to by the steam locomotive which frequently pulls the train. During the trip, the train passes over the Glenfinnan Viaduct, a twenty-one arched bridge constructed between 1897 and 1901. With each of the arches spanning fifteen meters and a maximum height of thirty meters it is an impressive sight, and the viaduct is probably most famous now from the Harry Potter films, which used it for the scenes featuring the Hogwarts Express.

The viaduct itself is however a feat of engineering due to it being constructed entirely from concrete with no additional strengthening added, and it was one of the largest tasks undertaken using concrete at the time. It is this construction method that leads to a story of the bridge being haunted. In order to build the bridge, shuttering had to be first constructed and concrete poured in to form the massive pillars that support the arches. This was achieved by using carts loaded with concrete, pulled by a horse. The cart would be backed up to allow the concrete to be poured into the shuttering, and legend has it that during this process, one of the carts toppled backwards into the concrete, taking the horse and its driver with it. They all promptly sank into the several meter deep pool of wet concrete, and are said to remain buried within the viaduct pillar to this day. Reports of strange lights and noises around the base of the viaduct have been made, leading to the belief that this is the workman re-enacting his final actions that ultimately led to both his own death and that of his horse.

Fort William Library

Fort William Library stands at the end of the main street, close to the railway station, on a site where for over three hundred years a tree stood that was used by the Governors of the fort to hang wayward clansmen. In the 1970s the tree was cut down to make way for the construction of the library. Some locals warned that cutting down the tree would bring bad luck to the town. Shortly after the library was opened, staff arriving in the morning found the door open, books thrown all over the place, and the sound of dogs were heard inside the building. Unoccupied toilets are also have said to have flushed themselves.

Incidents continue to happen and a number of unexplained light anomalies have turned up in photographs of the area, so it is possible that cutting down the tree disturbed the spirits of those who lost their lives there.

Delgatie Castle, Aberdeenshire

The current Delgatie Castle comprises of a tall tower house, which dates back to the 16th Century, with later side additions including a chapel, added around the 18th Century. An earlier one is thought to have stood on the site previously, possibly dating back to the 11th Century, but nothing remains of this.

The castle had started to fall into a state of serious disrepair by the start of the 20th Century, and was used as army barracks during the Second World War and then abandoned, allowing the decay to continue until Captain John Hay set his sights on it and put together a plan for its restoration. The castle had originally become the property of the Clan Hay after the Battle of Bannockburn in 1314 and Captain Hay wanted to restore it to its former glory as a Clan Hay centre for future generations. Numerous specialists and architects advised him that the castle was beyond repair, but he ignored their advice and proceeded with the renovation. Without his determination, it is almost certain the castle would have been lost.

The castle, which has the widest turnpike stair in the country, is now a four-star tourist attraction with bed and breakfast facilities. It is operated as a non-profit organisation with all the proceeds being used for the upkeep of the castle. Many of the original features have been restored, including impressive painted ceilings, and it has a more homelike feeling rather than the 'colder' feel some castle have.

One of the bedrooms is reported to be haunted by a woman with red hair who seems to take some enjoyment in frightening people. The ghost has been given the name Rohaise and only seems to appear when men are staying in the bedroom. It is claimed she was seen many times during the time the soldiers were there in the Second World War, probably due to them all being men, and it is said that one occasion an entire group of soldiers fled the castle when Rohaise appeared to them. Little information is available as to her identity, but it is thought she may have been one of those responsible for protecting the castle, a role she continues to do to this day by scaring people away.

The castle is also said to be haunted by a monk, who first appeared after the daughter of one of the castle owners dreamt about a body being hidden in the wall of one of the rooms. She must have been insistent with her story, and it seems the wall was checked and a skeleton in a crouched position, along with the remains of some black cloth clothing, were found. It is believed the ghost may be Joseph Hay, who was a monk who returned to the family home during the Scottish Reformation in the 16th Century, a time when the monasteries were being destroyed and monks killed. Joseph would have been able to continue to practice his religion in the privacy of the castle and, after his death, the decision had been made to bury him within the castle walls. As the sightings of the phantom monk increased, it became apparent something had to be done and a local minister was asked to perform an exorcism, after which all reports of sightings of the monk ceased.

When visiting the castle, the curator also told me that Captain Hay himself haunts the castle, guarding the door and preventing anyone he feels is untrustworthy from entering. I have taken many photographs during visits to the castle, but have yet to capture anything unusual. The chapel however does have a strange feel to it, perhaps Joseph Hay has not yet left but is choosing not to show himself.

The House of Terror. No.17, Edinburgh

The house known most commonly simply as Number 17, was situated in the Inverleith/Silvermills area of Edinburgh, close to the botanical gardens. It became known for having something within one of the attic rooms, which left those who ventured there terrified. Owners would hear noises from the room when it was unoccupied, yet when they went to check they would find the room in total darkness and silent, with no explanation for the noises. The room constantly had an unwelcoming feeling and eventually no one would go into the room. Unable to deal with the constant unexplained occurrences and the bad feeling in the house, it was eventually abandoned by its owners, and despite standing in one of the most desirable areas of the city, because of the rumours of some evil spirit occupying the attic room it stood empty for many years.

In the early 1800s, a young couple that were not put off by the rumours saw the potential the property offered, so they purchased it and turned the property into a guest house which became known simply as 'Number 17'. Almost immediately people staying in the attic room started to report strange incidents, and some even refused to enter the room. One of the housekeepers is said to have screamed loudly while in the room and fled in a state of panic. After she had recovered, she refused or was unable to speak of what she had seen in that room that had so terrified her.

With rumours once again circulating, the owners grew anxious about the effect it would have on their business, and so when they were approached by a young man called Andrew Muir, who offered to stay the night in the room to try to find out what was really happening, they jumped at the chance. Andrew was a student in the city with deep religious beliefs, and it was these beliefs rather than a 'daredevil attitude' that had led him to make his offer. Arrangements were made and the owners only had one stipulation that Andrew had to agree to. They insisted he had a bell in the room with him, and if anything happened or he needed assistance he was to ring the bell to alert the owners, who would come to his aid.

Andrew retired to the room for the night and, as all was quiet for several hours, the owners also retired for the night. Around 2am the bell ringing and a loud scream from the room awakened them. They rushed to young Andrews's aid, but found him lying dead on the bed, with the bell by his side. His eyes were said to be wide open and he had a look of sheer terror on his face. Following the incident no one would enter that room again, and the guesthouse eventually closed. The row of houses in which it stood was demolished a few years later and the truth of what lurked in the house was lost forever.

The Royal Mile, Edinburgh

The street commonly known as the Royal Mile is actually a series of streets that run from Edinburgh Castle at the top to the Palace of Holyrood House at the bottom. It is probably the most famous street in Edinburgh and a major tourist destination, attracting thousands of visitors to see the ancient buildings, quaint and unusual shops and many street entertainers. Looking into the history of the area however reveals a dark past.

A headless drummer who is seen standing high on the castle walls playing his drums haunts Edinburgh Castle. According to legend, a sighting of the drummer is a warning that the castle is about to be attacked and fortunately, he has not been seen for a very long time.

Further down the Royal Mile many locals can be seen spitting openly in the street, an action that often offends those who witness it. There is however very good reason for this unsavoury act. Anyone looking down at the ground at this point will see a heart formed in the street, the Heart of Midlothian;

The Heart of Midlothian

The Heart of Midlothian marks the spot for the entrance of the old tollbooth prison. The building was hated by locals as it was the place where taxes were collected and later where prisoners were held prior to being hanged at the gallows, which stood a short distance away. People initially started to spit on the door of the building as they passed to show their dislike of the tax collectors, and the tradition continued once it was a prison. However, people now started to spit on it to show not only their opinion of the building, but also to show they hoped never to be held in the squalid conditions inside or be marched out of the door to the gallows. When the building was demolished in 1817 the tradition continued. As there was no longer a door, people began to spit on the street at the point where the door once stood, marked by the Heart of Midlothian. Today it is considered good luck to spit on the heart.

The lower half of the Royal Mile is often missed as people tend to walk from the castle to the South Bridge, which is about half way down, and then across to the city centre. It is worth continuing down the Royal Mile, not only for the architecture but also for more macabre sites.

At the bottom of the Royal Mile stands Queensberry House, which is now incorporated as part of the Scottish Parliament building. Originally it was a grand house, constructed in the late 17th century and home to William Douglas, 1st Duke of Queensberry. Following his death in 1695 the property became home of his eldest son, James, 2nd Duke of Queensberry. James was an unpopular man in Scotland due to accepting a substantial sum of money to help push through the Treaty of the Union, which ultimately led to the Act of the Union in 1707, joining the Kingdoms of Scotland and England. Indeed, it was while campaigning for this that a horrific incident is claimed to have occurred in the house.

James's eldest son, also called James, was said to be insane and violent, which led to him being kept locked in a room in the house. James senior had to retain bodyguards that he took with him for protection whenever he left the house, and while his father was out trying to gain support for the Treaty of the Union accompanied by all of these guards, young James had been left alone in the house. Somehow he managed to escape and is reported to have found a servant working in the kitchen, whom he proceeded to attack, roast alive on the kitchen spit roast, and then start to eat before being found by his returning father. The oven where it was claimed the servant was roasted is still in the house, and his agonising screams have been heard on many occasions within the building.

The Palace of Holyroodhouse at the bottom of the Royal Mile is said to be haunted by the ghost of Agnes Sampson. Agnes was a healer and as a result she was accused of witchcraft in the late 16th Century. She was subjected to horrific torture, including the witch pricker, starvation, being 'walked' and refused sleep, all in an attempt to gain a confession. She showed remarkable resistance, resulting in her suffering being prolonged with increasingly sadistic methods being used, until eventually she gave in and made a confession to end it. She was strangled and burned at the stake. Her bald, naked ghost has been seen wandering through the grounds of the palace.

About half way along the Canongate section of the Royal Mile sits Canongate Kirk and Kirkyard (church and churchyard). Dating back to the late 17th Century, the kirkyard is the final resting place for many well-known figures in world history, including one connected with the Palace. A plaque marks the part of the kirkyard where the body of David Rizzio is said to have been placed. Rizzio was the private secretary to Mary, Queen of Scots, and was murdered in the queen's apartments in Holyroodhouse, in front of the heavily pregnant queen by a gang of noblemen. It is strongly believed that the queen's husband, Lord Darnley, who had grown jealous of the relationship between Mary and Rizzio, ordered the murder and may have taken part in the slaying. It is said bloodstains still mark the spot of the murder, and all attempts to remove them have been unsuccessful.

It is however a fictional character that is probably the most well-known name. Charles Dickens is said to have visited Edinburgh to present a lecture and during this visit he walked through Canongate Kirkyard, where he saw a memorial with the inscription 'Ebenezer Lennox Scroggie – Meal Man'. The words 'Meal Man' referred to Scoggie's occupation as a corn merchant, but Dickens misread the inscription as 'Mean Man' and thought it was a strange thing to put on a memorial. This thought seems to have stayed with him as two years later, when he published what is probably his best-known novel 'A Christmas Carol', the main character was Ebenezer Scrooge, referred to as a 'mean man'.

Although I am not aware of any specific ghost stories relating to the kirkyard, it is an interesting place and several of the organised tours do use the kirkyard to add to the atmosphere when telling the tales of horror that once occurred in old Edinburgh. It was during a visit to there that I captured what I consider to be one of my best photographs;

Orb at Canongate Kirkyard

Anyone looking at this photograph could quite rightly consider it to be yet another orb photo, and it is correct that it is a photograph of an orb. What impressed me about this particular photograph is that it was taken in full daylight, with no flash. I was preparing to take a photograph of the open mausoleum when I saw the orb form and grow within the chamber before floating out and past me through the viewfinder of the camera, which is something I cannot explain.

The Canongate's connection with graves does not end with the kirkyard. The area also has connections with the infamous mass murderers, Burke and Hare. Although commonly known as grave robbers, Burke and Hare did not actually rob graves - they used other methods to acquire their bodies. The two Irish labourers first met when Burke moved into a boarding house, which was owned by Hare. In 1827, one of the lodgers known as Donald, died. He owed Hare rent money at the time of his death and to recover the money, which

64

had been lost, Burke and Hare came up with a plan to sell his body to the local medical college. At the time, colleges needed bodies for learning and teaching but were limited to the use of bodies of criminals who had been executed, which were often in bad shape. Burke and Hare were therefore well rewarded for their clean, fresh body that they were able to provide. When another of the lodgers at the property became ill, Burke and Hare took it upon themselves to assist him to his demise by covering his nose and mouth while restraining him by leaning on his chest, leading to death by suffocation with no marks or damage to the body itself. Again, they were well paid for the body.

Seeing a way to make easy money, Burke and Hare started to lure people to the house where they would be encouraged to drink heavily, before being suffocated in the same manner as the first victims (a method now known as 'Burking' after the pair). At least one of their victims, Mary Paterson, was lured from the Canongate. Mary, along with her friend Janet Brown, were taken from the Canongate to a house in the adjoining Gibb's Close, which was owned by Burke's brother. Mary passed out, probably due to too much drink, but Janet remained sober and left, saying she would come back for Mary later. When she did return, she was told Mary had left earlier with Burke, however, the reality was that Mary lay dead in the house, waiting to be taken to medical college.

When Burke and Hare were caught a year later, they are known to have killed at least sixteen people, although the final number is probably higher. Both blamed each other for the killings and, because they had always been very careful to select victims who would not be missed, the authorities had little evidence to work with. Eventually a bargain was struck with Hare whereby he gave evidence against Burke and, in return, he was freed. Burke was hung in January 1829 in front of a crowd estimated at around twenty five thousand people. Ironically, his body was passed to one of the medical schools for dissection, and his skeleton remains on display at the University of Edinburgh's Anatomy Museum. Further up the Royal Mile, at the Police Information Centre in the High Street section, one of the more macabre 'souvenirs' from their murder spree remains on view. A business card case sits in a glass cabinet, which does not look unusual in itself until you read the description that reads;

'This small business card case is made from the left hand of William Burke who was hanged in 1829. The judge decreed that as part of his sentence Burke's body be used by the School of Anatomy at Edinburgh Surgeons Hall. The skin was removed from Burke's body and used to make several items.'

The connection with Burke and Hare and the Canongate continued after Burke's death. In 1836 some boys were hunting rabbits on a hill known as Arthur's Seat, situated in Holyrood Park at the bottom of the Royal Mile, and found seventeen miniature coffins in a cave on the hillside. They were stacked within slate, and the varying levels of decay indicated they had been placed there over a period of time rather than all at the same time. Inside each of the coffins was a tiny figure carved out of wood, fully clothed and with detailed faces. With no explanation for the purpose of the coffins or why they were there, speculation started that they were connected with the notorious killers.

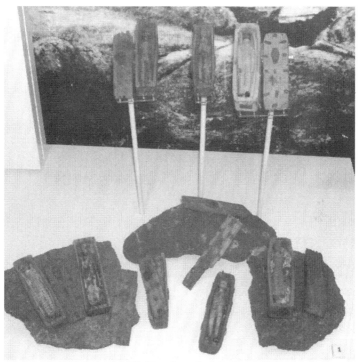

Miniature Coffins found at Arthur's Seat

The reason for bodies for the surgeons to dissect being so scarce was due to the belief at the time that if a body was denied a burial, the spirit could not move on and would remain on the earth. People were therefore unwilling to donate their body to medical science for fear this would trap their spirit. The bodies of executed criminals were used because it was deemed that the crimes that had led them to be executed already denied them the right to a burial. It is therefore considered that the coffins could contain the effigies of the pairs' victims (the first body that they snatched from before it could be buried and the sixteen they are known to have murdered), indicting that Burke and Hare feared the

67

possibility that their victims could return to seek vengeance. Thus, they had the effigies made and buried them in the cave in an attempt to appease their spirits. If this was the purpose of the coffins, it doesn't appear to have worked as there are numerous reports of shadow figures being witnessed in the narrow closes and lanes which extend from the Royal Mile, leading to the belief that these may well be the spirits of some of Burke and Hare's as yet unidentified victims.

The coffins were passed into a private collection and some have completely disintegrated. The remaining coffins are on display at the National Museum of Scotland in the Cowgate area of the city, a few minutes walk from the Royal Mile.

Loch Ness and the Monster

View of Loch Ness

Reports of a monster lurking in the water of Loch Ness, Scotland, date back as far as the 6th Century when St Columba is said to have come across a group of Picts burying a man at the side of the River Ness. After they explained that a water beast had killed the man while he had been fishing, St Columba sent one of his companions out into the river to lure the monster up from the depths. When it appeared, St Columba raised his hand and drew the shape of a cross in the air while commanding the beast to stop its attack and never to harm man again. It immediately stopped and swam back down from whence it came.

Although there were many more reports of beasts at the Loch after this, Scottish mythology has many stories of creatures that lurk in or near to water, such as the Kelpie, a large, strong horse that was said to lure people down to the banks of rivers with an undeniable desire to

69

ride the horse. Once they were on its back, the Kelpie would charge into the water, drowning its victim before eating them. The early story of the Loch Ness Monster is therefore tied in with such mythology and it was not until 1933 that the monster in the form it is now known became popular.

In April 1933 Mrs Mackey, a local hotel manageress, was driving with her husband to Inverness when they spotted a large, black monster close to the top end of the Loch. Later, in July 1933, George Spicer was travelling along the banks of the Loch with his wife when they witnessed a large animal cross the road in front of them as it returned to the Loch. They described the animal as being approximately four feet tall and twenty-five feet long and having no distinguishable legs or feet. A similar incident occurred the following month when a young veterinary student called Arthur Grant claimed he nearly hit the beast when travelling home on his motorbike.

After these stories were reported, several other claims of sightings followed including what was believed to be the first ever photograph of the monster, taken in November 1933 by Hugh Gray. Mr Gray reported that while walking home from church he became aware of a commotion in the loch, and upon seeing something splashing about, he took out his camera and started to take photographs. Only one photograph shows what appears to be a creature on the surface of the water, but the image is so distorted it is difficult to take it as conclusive evidence of the monster.

The most famous photograph was taken the following year by Robert Wilson. The photograph clearly shows the image of the humped back, long neck and serpent-like head which is now so commonly associated with the Monster. The photograph gained considerable press coverage and became known as 'The Surgeon's Photograph' due to Wilson distancing himself from it and not wishing his name used. However, the use of the association with a surgeon in the title probably added to the validity as people deemed that someone in such a respected position would be morally responsible and unlikely to be lying about the photograph. Sadly, it transpired that the faith put in the occupation was misjudged when in 1994 Christian Spurling made a deathbed confession that the photograph was a fake. Spurling's step father was Marmaduke Wetherell, a respected big game hunter who, at the end of 1933, had been asked by the Daily Mail newspaper to hunt the monster and produce evidence of its existence. Wetherell subsequently found tracks at the Loch side that he claimed belonged to the monster, but when the photographs were published in the paper, experts at the National History Museum recognised them as being from a hippopotamus. At that time dried hippo feet were often used as umbrella stands, and someone in Wetherell's position would have easy access to one. The photographs were declared a fake and Wetherell was humiliated, and although it was not established whether he was responsible, or someone else had made the footprints and he had failed to correctly identify them, it cast doubt on his credibility amongst his peers. According to Spurling, his stepfather had asked him to make a realistic looking model of the monster in an effort to fool the paper. Spurling, who was a model maker, made the now famous monster shape and placed it on top of a toy submarine. They photographed the model in the Loch and then created cropped pictures to hide the small size of the monster. Robert Wilson was called in to front the hoax as a convincing individual with no connection to Wetherell. The photographs and the story around when Wilson supposedly took them were given to the Daily Mail, the same paper that had humiliated Wetherell the year before.

The surgeon's photo resulted in a boost in visitor numbers to the area and reports of sightings of the monster continued, the most recent sighting being in 2011 by the owners of a local store who spotted a large, black creature swimming through the water before disappearing. However, the question of what the monster is remains unanswered.

To fully consider the reports of a monster, it is necessary to appreciate the size of the loch. The loch is almost twenty-three miles long, over one a half miles wide at the widest point, and around 750ft deep. The loch holds more water than the total volume of water held in all the lakes in England and Wales combined. The Loch is therefore easily vast enough for a large creature to survive, and the number of sightings over the years indicates there is something there. Sceptics point to the increased number of sightings since 1933 as an indication of a scam to lure tourists to the area, particularly given that most sightings now occur in Urquhart Bay, which is overlooked by Urquhart Castle, one of the main tourist attractions.

Urquhart Castle viewed from Urquhart Bay

This can however easily be explained as the road at the side of the Loch was completed in 1933, resulting in more people visiting. It is reasonable to expect that if there was something mysterious in the Loch, the more people that visit, the more frequently it will be spotted, and with Urquhart Castle having clear views over the bay and up the Loch along with many visitors, it is natural for a lot of sightings to be from the Castle.

This is however where the mystery starts to raise further questions, even for believers in the monster. With so many visitors, and the surface of the Loch being almost permanently covered in pleasure cruisers and smaller boats, why is the monster not witnessed more frequently and why are there not more photographs of it? There are of course numerous photographs that have been published over the years, but nothing clearly showing the creature. The effect of so many boats on the Loch's surface actually results in many of these photographs, where the wakes from the numerous boats collide with each other, creating unnatural swells and shapes in the water. Scientists have also demonstrated that the dark, peat filled water of the Loch is unable to maintain a food source for what would have to be a breeding pair of large creatures. Any creature would have to come in from the sea via the River Ness, which passes through Inverness, and it is very unlikely that a large creature in the relatively small river would go un-noticed.

There is however another possibility. Loch Ness lies in an area called The Great Glen, which is a natural fault line caused by the collision of two of the earth's tectonic plates millions of years ago. This collision effectively joined the top part of Scotland to the rest of the country. The fault line however extends well beyond the coast of Scotland. It is estimated to extend from close to Ireland, cutting through the edge of the Isle of Mull off the west coast of Scotland and on beyond the north east coast as far as the Shetland Isles, a distance of around 300 miles. The fault continues at Shetland as the Walls Boundary fault and to the west it connects to fault lines through Ireland and onto the Mid-Atlantic Ridge, which was formed later and cuts the fault line in two. There have been suggestions for many years that there may be underground caves and caverns that feed into Loch Ness, and this was added to with the discovery in the 1980s of deep caves in Urquhart bay. The caves go to a depth of 812 feet, around 60 feet deeper than the Loch was previously believed to have been, and these caves had not been detected in earlier sonar scans of the Loch, which means there could be more not yet discovered. The caves earned the name 'Nessie's Lair' or 'Nessie's Cave' with many speculating that they may lead to deeper caverns. This raises questions as to whether there could be a series of as yet undiscovered caves leading up through the fault lines and out to sea, which would allow a large creature access to the Loch.

Over 90% of the world's oceans are unexplored, and as we start to explore more, discoveries are being made of previously unknown species of sea life, or species that had been believed to be extinct. It is therefore possible that the Loch Ness Monster is indeed one of these creatures, which travels undetected through underground caverns. The peat in the water would prevent it from being seen when at depth (bear in mind numerous unexplained objects have been detected on sonar). The depth of the Loch creates an unusual situation where the Loch never freezes over. The top 100 feet of water in the Loch varies according to the weather, but below that the water is constant at around 44 degrees Fahrenheit (about 6.6 degrees centigrade). Indeed perhaps it is only when weather conditions are suitable, raising the temperature of the top layer of water, that the creature rises to the surface, hence very intermittent sightings as it would require the correct weather conditions at the same time as one of the creatures was in the Loch.

I do not believe the monster is any form of plesiosaur as many think, I do however believe there is some form of large creature, probably an eel, much larger than those which have been found so far, which at least occasionally visits the Loch, possibly via the means described above.

Note from the Author

I hope you have found the information contained in this book interesting. As stated at the start, I am in no way trying to influence the reader's decision on the validity of any ghost stories and my intention was solely to present the history, reported hauntings where there are any, any photographs I have and my personal opinion.

The following books by the same author are also available.

Scotland's Hidden Hauntings

Scotland is well known for being one of the most haunted countries in the world, but alongside the famous locations are many less well-known places, with equally eerie and horrific stories.

What really lurks in the underground streets of Edinburgh and why is a section of an ancient graveyard in the City kept locked? What really happened during the witch trials at the start of the 18th Century? Who is in the phantom coach that thunders towards St Andrews on stormy nights and why do students at the town's world famous university avoid walking on an area of cobbled road outside St Salvator's Hall?

Although some of the better-known stories are touched on, this book focuses on the less well-known locations and rather than just re-tell the stories, the author has personally visited each site. Some are locations known to be haunted, in which case the book provides some history and details of the reported hauntings, along with the author's own experience and any unexplained photographs. Other locations are not known to be haunted but, when visiting, something unusual showed up in the photographs. For these locations, the book provides some history, the author's own experience and the unusual photographs.

Book 2 in the Haunted Explorer Series

Haunted Scottish Castles and Houses

Journey through the beautiful countryside of Scotland, and it won't be long before you find a castle or grand manor house. Ranging from the fully restored magnificent homes and hotels to decaying ruins, each one has it's own unique history. With so many originally built for protection in far more violent times than today, it is not unusual to discover that behind the visually stunning exteriors can lie a dark and sinister past and the terrifying acts of cruelty that were carried out within the walls have resulted in tales of hauntings.

In this book the author explores a selection of these castles and manors, giving details of the reported ghostly happenings and the history of the property which helps explain why they are reputedly haunted. Many of the properties have been personally visited by the author allowing him to provide photographs and offer his own views and experiences.

Book 3 in the Haunted Explorer series.

Rise of the Witch (The Witch Hunter Series: Book 1)

In the year 1563, Mary, Queen of Scots, passed Scotland's Witchcraft Act. The act not only made witchcraft illegal, but to consult with or defend a witch was also illegal. And so the witch hunts began.

By the time the act was repealed in 1736, around 4000 ordinary people had been accused, tortured, convicted and executed. They were all innocent.

Or were they?

When Peggy Stuart learned that she shared her name with a notorious witch from the witch trials of the late 1600s, she felt the need to find out more information. Little did she know that her actions would lead to the resurrection of the witch, who has lain dormant for over 300 years waiting for the day she would be released to once again unleash her powers on an unsuspecting world.

Finding that modern weapons are useless and unable to control the witch, drastic action is considered by the government to try to stop her. Peggy and her partner, Matt Taylor, a historian at the local university and an expert in mythology, must work together to try to discover the truth behind what really happened during the witch trials. Only then can they find a way to stop the witch and avoid the catastrophic event being planned by the authorities.

Their investigation leads them to shocking discoveries about the past, and the present, which will forever change the world as we know it and thrust them into a new life where they must fight to preserve and protect.

Gateway Manor

After being abandoned for ten years following a failed renovation attempt and a mysterious death, work on Gateway Manor has started again, this time with the assistance of a television show called 'Renovating Ruins'. As work progresses, the secrets of the imposing mansion house are slowly revealed and an ancient evil which has lain dormant within the manor for centuries is disturbed and released, trapping everyone within the building. Members of the television show crew, assisted by a stranger with ties to the property must work together to stop the beast from escaping the walls of the manor.

Coming Soon:

The Haunted Explorer – Book 4

Further explorations of haunted locations throughout Scotland

Battle of the Witches: Book 6 in The Witch Hunter Series

After a quiet period of time, there seems to be an escalation in the activity of strange happenings. Matt and Peggy are asked to find out what is behind this increase in activity and make a shocking discovery.

Book 6 will be a full length novel, bringing the current series to a conclusion.

Zombie Colony – Europe

An incident on a remote Norwegian island triggers a series of events resulting in an apparently imminent zombie apocalypse. A botched government attempt to contain the outbreak brings the apocalypse closer. With parts of Europe now a no-go area and deemed zombie colonies, the governments of the UK and USA must work together to contain and stop the spread before the whole of Europe and beyond is engulfed.

For updates on these and other books, please check out my blog at http://gstewartauthor.com/

About the Author

Greg first became interested in the paranormal when his parents took out a subscription for him in 1980 for a magazine entitled 'The Unexplained'. Since then he has read numerous books on the subject, visited many reported haunted sites and taken part in investigations.

His interest in all things paranormal led him to start to write short fiction. He has recently finished a book exploring less well known haunted locations based on personal experiences and is developing at least one of his short stories into a full length fictional novel.

Greg's recent Witch Hunter series is gathering pace and there is around 4 novelettes planned for the series, before the final novel to conclude the series. At that point it is possible the series will be continued or a planned prequel series will be launched.

As a keen explorer of historical buildings and sites, Greg has recorded numerous tales of hauntings and had several as yet unexplained experiences himself. Some of these have been complied into the book 'Scotland's Hidden Hauntings', a collection of less well known haunted locations in Scotland. He is currently working on a second real ghost story book.

For more details, to view some photographs taken during visits to haunted locations please visit his website at:

http://gstewarthorror.weebly.com/index.html

Printed in Great Britain
by Amazon